Shepherd's Hour

Rikki Santer

LILY POETRY REVIEW BOOKS

Praise for *Shepherd's Hour*

Rikki Santer's *Shepherd's Hour* is full of surprises: an anachronistic shepherd crouching "among low bleats," a Rabbi's Jewcat, a flamingo menorah (my sister would like one,) a luscious warm bagel shepherding the speaker home though a scary night and described in such detail I ate of it too, and thoughtful art poems with engaging backstories. This is how culture warms, feeds, protects, and lives inside us. So many mishpocha brought to life in these pages: brave immigrant grandparents, Chiya, Rikel, Isac, Joseph, Uncle Saul, Uncle Lenny, and beat-kisser Auntie's Jewish humor transcending death via gravestone. We taste memories of savory mouth-watering deli and home-cooked meats, from a vegetarian poet no less, as well as grief for the beautiful capable mother too soon lost. What to do with the epigenetic fear represented here: yearning for a Golem protector when embers of antisemitism flare, memories of the historical ruptures of Shoah, pogroms on back through time? Apply them, dear reader, to human suffering wherever it occurs, both then and now, for in the particular lies the universal, and all who suffer yet aspire, as Malamud suggests, are "Jews."

Charlene Fix author of *Jewgirl*

"Sometimes we are simpering wounds/ sometimes prayer/ the sugar and salt of memory." So says Rikki Santer in her newest collection, *Shepherd's Hour.* Indeed, these poems are sweetly seasoned with blintzes, butter cake, deli fare, and Manischewitz, along with other familiar ingredients and talismans from Jewish culture and tradition. But more importantly, we also witness her grieving lost family members and artistic heroes, as well as grappling with personal and generational scars. In this time and moment, I deeply appreciate how Santer both relishes and interrogates her connection to Judaism.

—Hannah Stephenson, author of *In the Kettle, the Shriek*
    and *Cadence*

What do we get from a poet blessed with a deep memory and rich imagination, whose "mother turned her dreidel paperweight to gimel so everyone could win", and who inherited a cookbook that is a "midrash with/grandmother marginalia in Yiddish"? Yes, the poems are that rich, that originally singular. I could go on quoting from them and still want to quote more. So much to love and admire in *Shepherd's Hour:* the way Santer's language can shift and combine a lyrical storytelling with a Chagall-like surrealism, the expansive depth and richness of her Jewish sources, from freshly imaginative visions of the familiar (ancestry, the Golem, Lilith) to a retrieval of the (to me) too-forgotten, as in "Love Letter from Ghetto Girl Comedians to 21st Century Offspring," in which she reminds us of Patsy Abbott, Belle Barth, and Pearl Williams. Though a vegan, Santer still reserves a core in her Jewish soul for that delicious brisket, that nostalgia for the spiritual meat. Who wouldn't want to be a cockroach on the wall of Golda's party that invited all those lovely Biblical women warriors to their communal feast? I'm overwhelmed by Santer's expansiveness that can embrace the historical/cultural Judaic mishmash, from Jewcat to Leo Frank, from her Uncle Max's diner to Soutine's pointillistic paintings. Santer's influences are prodigious (many are named in "Shepherd's Cento") but *Shephard's Hour* collects a distinctive and delightful herd: radical, brilliant, soul-deep in heart-throbbing intelligence, outrageously Jewish, and ultimately singularly human. Santer's shepherd soul will feed your poetry sheep to full.

—Philip Terman, author of *The Whole MIshpocha: New and Selected Jewish Poems, 1998-2023* and *My Blossoming Everything*

"…So no one guesses that under your clothes you're a brave shepherd girl who climbs trees and chases away wolves with your staff."
Johanna Sinisalo, *The Core of the Sun,*

"From inside the pot on the stove someone
threatens the stars with a wooden spoon.
Otherwise, cloudless calm. The shepherd's hour."
Charles Simic, *The World Doesn't End:*

Also by Rikki Santer:

Front Nine: A Biography of Place
Clothesline Logic
Fishing for Rabbits
Kahiki Redux
Make Me That Happy
Dodge, Tuck, Roll
In Pearl Broth
Drop Jaw
Head to Toe of It
How to Board a Moving Ship
Stopover
Resurrection Letter: Leonora, Her Tarot, and Me
Zebra Lashes

For Sammy and BeeBee, still my divining rods for joy and purpose.

TABLE OF CONTENTS

Zemirot

I could be a raspberry torte cake, an embroidered bejeweled bimah, a
bobble-headed Shylock, a tattooed ghost with ribcage-wrought. How
to pasture where I'm from. Luna moth blown from the shaggy bark.
Tribe of dancing aphids powdering branches. Grandma cradled a tiny
klezmer band in her apron. Uncle assembled a flamingo menorah in
his front yard. I imagine Anne Frank's shepherd crook leading me
to safety in her sheepfold. Mother turned her dreidel paperweight to
gimel so everyone could win.

Suburban Trajectory

do you remember the time I sat at your parents' polished mahogany table in their crystal dining room while they whispered about me in their gleaming kitchen with a marble island way bigger than my mother's apartment kitchenette and I thought I heard *wayward upbringing* and *Jesus killers* before they joined us with their strained smiles and heaping platter of breakfast bacon / or at the cafeteria's lunch table when the unwrapping of my matzo peanut butter sandwich made my ligaments twitch in the cross-hairs of all your smirking eyes / or your *kike kike kikes* in so many different high school bathrooms / yet the shame was for my suburban sheltering like when in the back of a college classroom during a lecture on Celan I dissolved from my body to the ragged stench of a Dachau barracks and among the sunken faces was mine and when I returned I found each of you staring at my tear-stained cheeks / so in this category of my making I've been led by a trail angel to find myself circumnavigated by guilt-in-luck to remind myself of the tattoo buried deep into the flesh of my Hebrew school teacher's arm as it danced before her eager chalkboard

From Sister Namesake

Lost brother is that you
pulling invisible threads
after three days of heartbeat?
Your birthdate buried,
your gravesite suppressed,
but your name shaped mine;
I was next in line.

Now lifetimes have passed
and I ache for a shibboleth
that will release you
to sit across my table
as we roll down soft hills
of laughter and harvest stories
faceless but cued.

You are out there
in my steps, my turns,
in syllables that label
me you. Dare I craft
the sequel of your short
biography with base pairs
we share?

Was that you behind the fern
in our family portrait, you who
chipped the dinnerware, who
kidnapped orphaned socks?
Did you draw that eerie
moon the night our father
died or coaxed our mother's
whisper through the sunshine
of her funeral?

So strange to be here
without you, the stranded
uncle and brother-in-law
of you. Tonight I bathe
in the sleepless opera
of starlight and dare tidings
of dream state and return.

Shofar

The ram's horn carries fire from
camp to camp. I am camped deep,
shoulders into shoulders in a packed shul
on the High Holidays. Two mornings,
two evenings. My father's damp palm
as he holds my hand during each service.
I'm home from college, stand-in
for my bed-ridden mother. Raw horn.
No mouthpiece. Pure breath that launches
one steady blast. The shofar's tribal
question mark penetrates across centuries.
My father squeezes my fingertips. Our faces
turn to each other, eyes moist, heads nod.
Then three broken notes, quivering staccato,
and one long blow. High above the bimah,
from the choir chamber, a woman with
lustrous silver hair and a Stradivarius
delivers the haunting melody of Kol Nidre.
My father whispers she is the one who
introduced him to my mother. Papa
here with me at synagogue, stained
fringes of his prayer shawl, sanctuary
vibrating with atonement. Mother
at home with decaying nerve fibers,
plate of apple slices and honey in her lap.

> On this clear sky Rosh Hashanah morning,
> I crouch in the shade of a pin oak placing
> smooth stones on my parents' headstones
> keeping their souls in my world—my world
> without synagogue, without ram's horn,
> without the flame of certainty flickering
> in the ether.

Vegan Dreams of Meat

From the cabin we watch a wide
waterfall on the lip of our property
spill and spill its blood of red clay.
A hard rain has fallen all day.
Around the dinner table my father
and mother now decades dead
join us for a brisket that I think
I've left too long in the oven. I reach
for plates from the cupboard, a chipped
stack instead of my mother's Desert
Rose china. The carving knife slides
through generous layers of fat. No peas,
no carrots, no roasted potatoes to accompany,
just plump and juicy muscle that slips
obediently from its bones that I pass
to my smiling parents as the scene
dissolves out of focus, held hostage
by steam, the salt.

Leavings

Her wobbly handwriting in signature purple ink
on the face of a tiny envelope under perfumed
hankies—*7 extra pearls for choker.*
A hidden survivor in the nursing home drawer
where the velvet box was stolen, now nacre
of her leaving.

They wanted her belongings out before the funeral,
so in haste we harvested mostly chaff into paper
ream cartons—frayed sweaters, worn slippers, stash
of newspaper comic strips to be mailed to her minions.

But the irritant she regretted to leave behind,
this mother, high priestess of accessory,
was the memory of her mourning that loss
of pearl necklace by a faceless thief
she probably saw most days after.

Pearl necklace, favorite gift from my father who left
too early, Chanel No. 5 that lingered on each lustrous
bead after so many cha cha nights they spent together,
and her master plan—that a strand's legacy
would continue around the neck of her only daughter.

Seven orphaned pearls sucked from the shell
of maternal desire now returned to their browning
envelope to nestle with sachet and folded tongues
of my scarves for a life still detached but tethered.

Hide & Seek

I see you hiding there where I am hiding.
I am hiding in "I see you there."
            from "The Diary of a Golem" by Rodger Kamenetz

We scurried in all directions as if horsebeats
of the Cossacks were coming, and our cackles
assaulted every frequency of our childscape—
dense tree canopies and warped sidewalks
with stumbling stones. Sharp looks from
neighbors distant as planets, dark groans
from the man of the fancy house who liked
spitting tobacco juice at our toes. A swastika
wrist at 7-Eleven where our pennies got us
Lemonheads and Shockers. Local librarian
with smeared lipstick, *Try this one,*
her trembling hands and liver spots
pushing toward us Wisniewski's *Golem,*
her left forearm of blue numbers.
Sturgeon moon that August night.
We fell in love with medieval magic
and collaboration with the stars. Flashlights
under our chins, we crouched between boxwoods
to whisper homemade prayers for calling forth
a Golem recipe and we swore we saw wreaths
of vapor rising from the sandlot and a swinging
hulk capturing fireflies with heavy hands.
For weeks our anthropoid visited us in our
daydreams to slap pimpled tyrants in the lunch
line, to drain all the bottles from our parents'
liquor cabinet, to block their arguments before
they struck. Under the evergreen each night
we left him a friendship bracelet that we braided
cobalt and white from grandmother's embroidery
floss and each morning after breakfast it was gone.
Then algebra and biology induced us away
as the iris of construct closed in.

Shepherd's Hour

You've been a rusty parking lot for desolation
but this hour your night mind calculates
sheep bells deep in the belly of the ravine.

Your herd wanders through fog in syncopation,
their frosty breaths leave behind trails
of ellipses. You light another cigarette

and stumble down the steep hill of brambles
to crouch among their low bleats. Musk
of their matted wool drapes you in stillness,

stillness you're prone to making thick
with gloom and inertia. But this hour, listen
to the steadying of their hooves in high grass, place

your hands onto the rippling lilt of their haunches,
and taste the haunting vapors of hallelujah, so strange
to your lips, secret chord ready to release you.

How to Make a Picture Book For the Soul That You Miscarried

Fly by night and cover your eyes with ivy
Play hide and seek with the *God behind God*

Turn up the volume on that long rusty squeak
March into root-rough corridors that are narrow

Screech like a banshee
Murmur many sad hymns

Ride every wave of fur and feather
Get to know the rabbits and owls

Drink chai from a moon jar
Sauté everything you find naive

Backstroke in that cauldron of murky chowder
Fold every dry into wet to make a mercy batter

Lay on your back for hours pondering treetops
Fall in love again with waterfalls and creeks

Nevermind the minds of gale and whirlpool
Remember what fits into the palm of a newborn's hand

Seek those who need to come to dinner
Wonder for what's just over the brow of that hill

Believe that each next breath is your best
Give credence to the cleansing in scrawl and scratch

Bagel Lady in Night

Your role was banter and wisecrack in a stained apron under a proscenium string of lights crisscrossing the intersection of Court and Union. Relish your place in history, first street vendor in this college town, sidekick to Bagel Man and his buggy—and the occasion of your shift, when the bars began last call. A bagel should be defined by its hole, but these white-bread rolls had belly buttons in their paunches. Their shellacking of cream cheese and jam was manna for those cockeyed and stumbling—gummy carbs to soothe their souls. It's the replay of performance—the coven of ratty tie dye and drooping halter tops in their clouds of weed encircling you and your centrifugal force of timing and finesse. The tumble and clang of charcoal briquets into a dented, metal drum to keep the fire stoked, the bubble and sizzle of oleo oozing onto the grill, tapping of your tongs to the chorus of soured breaths slurring directives, glide of your maestra delivery of each and every warm treat in its waxed paper nest. And then that night heading home...smoke lingering in your hair, your fingers webbed with sticky sweat, you slip into an alley and midway the air halts, turns cold. You blink at what's above you, blue orbs floating in clusters. Your steps betray you on the bricked path, your breath shallow, quick. On each side, the hush and swirl of eerie syllables drizzle from the walls until you exit this portal onto the street. Pulled the next two blocks to your front door, your eyes are moist and your feet heavy with quagmire logic.

Crosshatching   *(after Maurice Sendak)*

Close your eyes / Have no fear
The monster's gone / He's on the run
and your daddy's here
> from "Beautiful Boy" by John Lennon

Imagination could stretch in these caves,
organize our world with flirty wonderhorn
our pockets brimming with tiny bells
our cloaks of tender cascades, folds upon folds.
O Wild, O Goose-step
O Dark Delectable,
O Right of Rain.
And you the accordion, Beautiful Boy
top-heavy & heavy-footed
with melodies that wickedly rhyme.
Please help me solve this poem.

How long I've been waiting to grow
out of so many jimmy-rigged somethings,
the weight of words, the dread that chafes,
narrow escapes from stews and stagnancies—
from heavy sets of thoughts
from the full load of who we are
from my mother's 1940 crimson copy
The Story of a Hundred Operas
tiny and tattered deep in my bedside bookcase.

My hand turns to overleaf—
your bare heels teasing piano keys
your Ragged Andy with inked heart,
your sock monkey with just one button eye,
the hubbub, the rumpus, the gaga
of you flying with fingernail wings
searching for the afikomen
in clefts & chasms—yet

memories no longer recognize you,
your dark clouds arming events.

Could we drop our plumb lines right into the heart of it
on the other side of moon
with incantatory words, embroider our story
puffs of dust under our running feet
the wagging tails of dreams
the lair of reveries for connective tissue,
inside with outside, outside with inside,
the wonder in rolling with surgical precision
a boiled egg beneath a knife blade
to release whole
its smooth and ready yolk.

Cradling Time

My grandparents from the old country I never met
or learned of those from further back, but I'm fond
of an aunt's story that my young Russian grandmother
whose name I carry, skated on the family pond and rode
bareback across fields with her longhair undone and airborne.

So I ponder. Did my first breath travel to tether and curl
around each letter in some ancient Hebrew manuscript
to claim a broken, unredeemed world? Is my DNA haunted
by someone who perished in pogrom or gulag [or]
whose timid hand reaching for a beer on a wooden table
in a Berlin cafe was pierced and pinned by knife
of a storm trooper [or] who frail and toothless,
refused to leave a cramped and drafty room
in an abandoned synagogue, yearning for just one
more serving of herring in oil with black bread
warm from the bakery in her radiant town now
pillaged [or] who brilliant in Yiddish theater
and the poetry of King Lear couldn't escape
bloody jaws of Soviet execution [or] who to survive,
pulled apart then burned naked bodies, flames flickering
from their Jude eye holes and buried his journal in a barrack
 to tell us so [or] who nervously hid yarmulke under a newsboy
cap to run errands outside the ghetto for ailing Bubbie [or]
who altered her name's "cumbersome" consonants
to play piano in the lobby of an American hotel with
signage: *no dogs or Jews allowed?* Today I may bristle

at the thin spit of a colleague's *jew him down,* the swastika
scrawled inside a turnpike bathroom, the antisemitic tweets
from celebrities or weep again and again for violent murders
impelled by domestic hate inside my own country, but I stand
guilty of a spectator's distance from the timeless and
insidious dusks aimed at my persistent tribe.

Of Steamship Steerage

in gratitude for my grandparents: Isaac Jacob, Chiva Rivka,
Joseph, and Rose—some time between 1903-1909

When America received you, your destiny
birthed mine two generations away.
You were remarkably immigrant yet
much of you is lost, so I project that
when you were decades younger than me now,
six months of brave decision eventually
jettisoned you from your shtetl. In stuffy offices,
your pale voices bribed and wheedled for tickets,
for passports, for tenuous itinerary to Atlantic.
It was hard to empty drawers. You gathered
only what could travel in leather trunk or
tattered pockets—favorite apron, embroidered
prayer shawl, pair of Shabbat candlesticks—
all for the day you squeezed and stumbled among
the masses scaling coarse gangplanks under
thin-soled shoes. In that next week or so,
with saltwater reviving your cheeks, you found
relief on deck from the stifling stench below of
too many bodies, and each day you read hope
in the muscular horizons of dawn or in the counting
of constellations. Angry waves sometimes stirred
your stomachs and non-kosher meals taunted
your bowels. In berths you slept in threadbare dresses
and overcoats after the sharing of whispered promises
soothed you under blankets of jute. In daylight you made
silence your second language and pushed up your wire
spectacles after each page of *siddur*. When footbridge
was finally lowered to the shores of Ellis Island, your legs
felt like furniture, your sighs released in cautious joy.
Then years later in Toledo or Irwin you sobbed
as you received word, from your Yiddish papers,
of the pograms back home—your tripwires of memory
for lost neighbors and friends not so fated as you.

Dear Chiva and Rikel

If somewhere there's a star chart that will lead me to you,
I would no longer lament you were never mine to keep.

Where are your grandmother stories that freight their magic,
hive of honey bees still busy in your soul, your head a

melancholy violin as I crouch into the wildflowers
outside your shtetl cottage, clouds like a school of

herring. Just a few strands from your hairbrush
now in my locket. Your jelly jar of buttons,

your red-leather-lined table, inlaid mother-of-
pearl belting its belly. Your butter cake

masterpieces, your feasts of pepperfish and tip-
of-the-tongue stews. You rub a hen's just laid egg

across your lips, keep seven cradles rocking
with your foot, herd gaggles of offspring under

clotheslines. Your daily allowance of a sliced-
in-half kalamata olive, silk stockings never

your allies but hairpins steadfast in the dark halls
of asthma and arthritis. You, phantoms of old age,

praying for dew each morning, and me,
forever hollow, Yahrzeit candle loyal,

wishing I had had a chance to kiss
the wrinkles around your knuckles.

Dear Isaac and Joseph

The black pointer with gold tip glides
like a finger, right to left, beyond what

the census shows and leaves me at the margins
of grandfathers whistling from front porches.

Breath-length memories I am too late for,
but for. No fingertips on my eyelids, no wooly

voice calling me to your lap. Yet, thistles punctuate
your greying beard of what you said when you fled

to heave your family from buckling Lithuanian
floors. The peddler algorithm of your honey

and brine bartering schmattahs door to door,
your American storefront stubborn for

closing on Sabbath. In your parlor, frayed
stacks of the Forward and socialist broadsides.

Bone dice in your pocket, pinochle in back
rooms. Late nights at the kitchen table, sitting

in the almost dark, you weep for Roosevelt,
draw in a braided wax taper to light your cigar.

Kosher

Her mother brought it with her
from across the ocean. Ancestry,
the mouth said to the kitchen.
Architect your space, so she did again
in her rust belt home. Later my mother
tried for awhile in her newlywed bungalow.
Filled the soup pot from the waterfall deep
in Lithuanian forests, segregated foodware
chipped by lineage of duty, revered
a tattered cookbook—midrash with
grandmother marginalia in Yiddish.

Then her ranch home in the suburbs along
with the chaos of American children.
Salted memory of loin, heart, warm snout—
slipped fast by knife glinted in science
of slaughter. The kosher butcher with little
paper boats mounded with raw hamburger
so fresh it tasted like sweet copper. Slippery
chicken livers sliding into the maw
of her meat grinder that she cranked
to the lyrics of showtunes. Eventually
breakfasts of pop tarts and bacon
in months populated by TV dinners.

Now it's Sunday in my kitchen
and as close as I get is a box
of kosher salt in the cupboard
and a tub of vegan butter in the fridge.
Sunlight curls over Mother's 1947
The Settlement Cook Book
(*The way to a man's heart*)
with fingerprint stains and ingredient
spatterings, all alphabet of her trying on

the mantle of homemaker. And tucked
between pages, handwritten recipes
in her signature purple ink, evidence
of her domestic invention. So tonight
will be her spice cake drunk on
Manischewitz from the year
she added it to everything—
her sultry meatloaf, her funny fish balls,
her lunchbox sandwiches gobsmacked,
one third peanut butter, two thirds grape jelly
tipsy with wine.

The Interfacings of Henry Miller and My Uncle Saul

At 95, Lt. Saul C.W.S., cradles a worn and dusty portfolio filled with ghostly footprints left by drunken typewriter keys and hurried ink that pace across browning postcards postmarked through the War months. It began with contraband, his mission atop the scuffed wooden planks of Gotham Book Mart on East 46th to purchase under the table a tropical classic bought *for the sex, of course.* Taped spine, vacant tea-stained cover, *imprenta de Mexico, 1940,* and months later three watercolor paintings by the same hands sent through the mail. The alchemy of correspondence from a barbaric yawp: Henry sprawls: *These paintings cannot be returned. Send me a check or money order for whatever you feel you can spare. You have to take a chance on me.* Then, <u>Murder The Murderer</u>: his war rantings arrive unsolicited with penciled marginalia: Send another $1.25 and beware *this air-condi-tioned nightmare.* Arrogance between the lines. The brazen young soldier returns one of the washes of the master and the sky tilts with insult and scolding. *Let the dead bury the dead. A writer must expect an occasional egg or tomato. You remember the parable of the doubting Thomas? Of course you may keep the other two watercolors—and with it goes (scot free) a bit of the sweat off my balls...*Decades pass. Saul lands a good wife, three well-versed kids, a retail business that delivers early retirement for world travel. On one excursion the roars of the sea lace Saul's unannounced knocks on the Big Sur door that per-turbs the napping bear and renders the encounter impotent. More decades pass. Saul as erudite grandpa then widower with *savoir faire.* The vibrancy of those two paintings survive, bathed by the ebb and flow of Pittsburgh light traveling through the panoramic windows of his downtown condo. Erect steeples in a cluster of crimson-roofed buildings float upon a bed of cobalt blue. And the portrait--Miller's mythic self smirking inside a swath of defiant red, framed by taunting curlicues--thick neck, crooked nose, a face poised askew to meet Lt. Saul's as he gazes across the many years singed with the aftertaste of an impromptu meal of regret.

When Auntie Kissed a Beat,

urban stew swizzled her tongue,
pastrami on warm rye arrested

any of her afterthoughts
of Wonder Bread dough balls

commandeered from crust.
His Luckies swiveled

between her fingers like
pipe dreams, so urbane,

so hip. Her thriftstore beret
dangled from the bedpost

while a shot, a toke, a snort
grew grammar in her mouth.

His kisses were swift and hard,
droplets of blood from her lips

were ellipses on napkins
of his poetry and for her

it was one subterranean,
nascent week, swaying

in lifestyle that bongoed
and bebopped her heart.

Then a crisp bus ticket,
dog-eared copy of *Howl*

left on her dresser, and a
story that grew plumper

each Thanksgiving until
a headstone put a period on it:

IF YOU CAN READ THIS,
YOU ARE STANDING ON
MY BOOBS, DIG?

You Were Here

for Uncle Lenny

The comfort in your diorama,
the heft of your hands.
Your thigh high boots, fringed purses,
nightgowns cotton & girly.
Gloopy fables off kilter,
captions in lipstick red.
Your timeline
never straight but loopy.
Your mossy stones lovesick
with pillowy coats
of rococo frosting.
Cosmic stews with
grit washed away
to pump up the kernels,
skies of smoked orange,
acorn thrones for pixies.
Water balloons
& flour bombs,
elegance of updo,
flashing nipples, the fluff
of your abundant,
double-barreled.
So full of zoom.
Everything beamed at you,
      brightly sour,
           minced sweet.

Uncle Max's Deli

Amen as we gather beneath the mantle of delicatessen where
the Marx Brothers held court in kippered herring barrels and I'll have
what she's having—a Danny Rose Special with marinara and cream
cheese. I scratch at the exfoliation of past before artisanal was deemed
artisanal, when his buckling linoleum and commas of grease tagged
foot-tall mountains of tender pastrami or humps of chopped liver
that bedded down with flirty romaine. How to surf these orbits
of memory that spin the halo of my vegan constellation. I am now
a distant galaxy away from splayed portions of smoked and salty flesh—
this fluorescent-bulbous moon where fat was prized and murder thrived
in thick display cases of bulging fish eyes and cow tongues moaning.
His deli was a movie set with perfect portions of schmaltz—dried
scraps of corned beef in ellipses around the slicer blade—dust balls
in the laps of empty front windows—a porcelain cityscape of plates
piled high on a steel counter—formica tables with just the right amount
of fade. I ain't kvetching about this concerto of tradition, this immigrant
fusion food I devoured gleefully on Sundays, ignorant of my people's ruse
of secret no-pork sausages during Inquisition or the thin and sour
rutabaga soup of Auschwitz. What sandwich would they name
after me now? A feeble union of smoked carrot lox and pureed
cashew shmear with a Mogen David martini to wash it all down?

Collector

> "Something of the lies and sadism will settle in the marrow of language. Imperceptibly at first, like the poisons of radiation sifting silently into the bone."
>
> *George Steiner, Language & Silence*

These days in apocalyptic video games we can choose to be the virus, like what lives inside his tower of boxes in this collector's comfortable suburban home. He's been buying and trading for two decades, but before he'll be shipping off his entire historical repository to a Polish museum, he sits me down at his dining room table. Plastic sleeves, then more and more of brittle Nazi text where the permeable membrane of fear breathes on. Figurines and ashtrays. Postcards and flyers. Twisted power of art. Talmudic passages perverted and betrayed. So many hooked noses suspended in propaganda urgency, atop teetering globes, spearing Aryans, embracing heaps of shekels. A smirking Mickey Mouse reshaped into dastardly Jude. Cunning hands big as hams. Shadowed contagion. Race debased. Rabbi lynched as sculpture. Slithering reptiles and parasitic spiders with Hasidic heads. On Reichsbank currency, stickers and banners *Do not buy from Jews!* Movie-style posters embodied by fat-lipped, gluttonous demons: *The Eternal Jew responsible for corruption of all humanity.*

Acknowledge this Jewish collector
alongside his cabinet
of curiosities packed
with chaos and abyss.

Witness his passion
as he tries to hold
a slippery history
by its spiked and bloody tail.

Jewcat

after Joann Sfar's *The Rabbi's Cat*

Parchment lives in my mouth and though
I haven't gobbled a parrot
as Sfar's feline, you still admire
the accordion between my ribs
as my chatter fills your bedroom.
I make you feel like Sunday,
my butterscotch fur your soft earth,
my warmth your pastry, honey-drenched.

In my primal gaze you are sometimes carcass
sometimes supplicant, so bring me
your lamb shank or gefilte fish in saucer.
And perchance I take a doze,
my skullcap and Cheshire grin
will levitate me so have ready
pomegranate seeds that I will lap up
from the orange blossom water
in your cup.

You know I know
how to best track in the long quiet
as I scrawl my many names
onto the shoulders of stars.
I lick the walls of alleyways
to the synagogue that's up on its feet.
Cat scratch fever has me wondering
if blood that clings to my whiskers
could ever be any sweeter.

Like that cartoon
Felix, I walk
with my hands
behind my back

my head down
deep in thought.
I am your rambunctious rabbi
revealing to you the through line—
it's better to remember
a few small things
because they help you measure
how much you don't know.

I insist that you add
to every fortune cookie fortune
the scripture *with the cat.*
And I remind you that I will never
carry your slippers
but my ancestral face will always carry
that shield of Maccabees.

And while I have your attention,
remember to honor my cousins—
Hello Kitty, Japanese princess
with no mouth commandeering
hives of color-drenched tchotchkes,
Tesla's glow-in-the-dark Macek
with his shower of sparks,
Schrödinger's figment of cat
who crouches in a quantum-ruled multiverse,
and Tom who spent his kitten years
as a tiny wandering Jew
before he met up
with that tref Jerry.

So at what point does history nod
back at us then turn platitude—
the right to remain
on Greek vases, in Egyptian tomb
paintings and Roman mosaics,

or as happy Asian paws mechanical
and beckoning? Am I not
Jew like you, transplanted
from civilization to civilization,
hungry for home?

What We Carry

for Judith Leiber, "The Bag Lady From Budapest"

Enter this immigrant tent
this—
halo of handbag
species of deadpan
long kiss in the hand
bejeweled creatures born from shtetl mud
       and green toolbox
minaudières that insist on themselves
beyond red carpet and manicured elite
sugar pixels
pebbled rinds
skins glazed to mirrored shine
grammar of luck for escaping
lexicon of polished belonging.

Celluloid Jewish

The homunculus wraps itself in a tiny *tallus*
and perches atop a projector whose light twists
a ragtime would-be cantor's blackface.

Folklore alchemy births a star embedded
into a chest while in flickering mist, pointed
hats, caftans, and beards storm the broken

gates of ghetto. Nazi focal length extends
to deliver more miniature Jews in secret
lavish rooms, pockets lined with Reichmark.

And then the gears of a liminal vessel carry
on an imperfect canon through the decades—
tender mise en scène of *Yom Tov* candles,

eggs dipped in salt around the table,
sentimental tempest of shtetl songs,
Hollywood celebrities scored cavalierly

to epic the bloody birth of nation, later
in concentric rinds of haunting memory
terrorists and avengers emerge from

both sides to prick the conscience
beyond what's flattened by news feeds.
Rebbe of deadpan and banana peel,

undercover *chasids*, aproned *yentas*,
soulless gangsters that thrive in vicious
chaos and corruption, or privileged

putzes pushed around by winds of angst.
All these braided textures of scorn and praise,
worlds in shorthand inflate and burrow

as we give ourselves to the aperture of it.
Portal fills with chorus of synthesizer, barking
dogs, shrieking voices all roiling just outside

the frame and the red, the red,
that little coat of red drifts
into a net of perpetuity.

My Friend's Chagalls

I'm thinking how paralyzingly delicious these blintzes are
that my dear friend serves me as I'm sitting in his dining room with his
mother's needlepoint tablecloth and Chagalls all around. A home gallery of
so many signed lithographs of little Jewish towns, their earthy darknesss and
chatty tones commingling with these fluffy Jewish cousins of crepes— O
bless higher content of butter and egg. And these blintzes would swallow
themselves if they could, surrounded by the centrifugal staccato of an
absence of gravity for floating roosters and floating cows, along with our
floating cherries quivering lush in sherry sauce. And I would marry these
blintzes if I could as they shimmer under swirling blues of moonlight, lovers
caressing and angels plump as dumplings all yoked to the magical ordering
of dreams. And my friend's eyes glisten, and my lips grin sticky sweet and
the fiddler and cello-goat serenade us as the genius
of Marc Chagall looks on, wise in the secret life of things.

Sway of Perennial

for T.M. Glass and her still life series, *The Audible Language of Flowers*
"To create a little flower is the labor of ages." William Blake

For some it's cars with status or football stats, but for me it's
the precision of what a naked table can launch with its puppetry

in eye lock. Her bouquets rhapsodize, hum into a sea of black velvet
as if they were poised on Pound's *wet, black bough.* Each antique

vase a proud mystic that summons blossoms teeming for my honeyed
hunger—all perfect pitch served lush. What could T.M.'s flower

anthologies be dreaming—azaleas, tulips, narcissus, bleeding hearts—
cut at their freshest, defying gravity, arranged into a superlative world?

Do they return to the brothel of a Queen Mother's pleasure garden, coy
for sex as they part their floral skirts? Do they savor the fractal surprise

of digital cultivation, botanical theatrics of trompe l'oeil, eternal lives
folded into golden mean? So here I am, dreaming, too, of my mother'a

rubber birds of paradise in her foyer's planter, dust coating their silence
but not their drama of entryway—and the wingbeats of orchids harmo-
nizing

atop the rim of her bathtub, the only room where east-facing sunlight
was best. For my wedding day she tried every florist in town for me

to carry calla lilies like a tender baby, a bouquet she had wanted for
her own day in her sister's tiny living room—no such flowers yet lustre

from her navy silk shirtwaist dress with rhinestone buttons that's now
wrapped and resting in my cedar closet. Morning arrives now outside

my bedroom window and I imagine tiny feet of black ants following
pheromone trails to tickle peony buds, matins for unlocking a profusion

of fuchsia—my mother's delicate pets that I transplanted here
from her long ago garden. Still lifes never silent, never still.

Packing with Lilith

Parked under a streetlight, Lilith finishes
her Lucky and tosses its butt out the window
of her oxblood Buick Riviera.
Her mindstage is seismic, the buzzing edge
of her looking deliciously full of herself.
What I'm saying is she doesn't care
if we think of her or not.
We walk arm in arm, our cobalt tresses
abundant and a Zig-Zagged joint between us,
feral in our adolescent Eden.

We wonder if she's been waiting for us.
Tonight we could be her hand-me-down
legends, another crop of invasive species.
Her spiked-heeled potions lace our nostrils,
her snake print coils around our torsos.
We began as obscure girls pranking
boots and mittens in school cloakrooms,
then graduated to sipping the sweet burn
of peppermint schnapp behind the strip mall.
In our matrix of imagined power,
we taunt a homeroom's teenaged mother
or post another night's rendezvous
with those sophomore guys from 7-Eleven,
rowdy hook and snag of zippers.

O Lilith, ghost of patriarchal notions,
first sister icon reclaimed by these sisters,
we imagine you straddling rabbis
of Talmud and Midrash while wedging
fish hooks into their quivering tongues.

Our voices trill like screech owls,
we are punk rock goddesses
dancing around a bonfire, clitorises
blooming in moonlight.
Not quite fiends, we like that judgment
will follow us home. But Lilith doesn't
acknowledge our waving as she tosses
her Macy's shopping bags
onto her front seat and lays down
the rubber like nobody's business.

Luthier

For the last two decades, Israeli Amnon Weinstein
has been locating and restoring violins that were
played by Jewish musicians during the Holocaust.

Of and not of the habit of terror. Each violin
a door to the many. The many. The barbed

accounts, these unsung bodies, in bereft immensity,
surrendered to a past that won't take them back.

In his workshop, the luthier planes the faces
of those hurled from cattle cars, buried under poppies,

human ashes still lingering in their inner chambers.
Each fragile restoration denounces the ribcage

of those gunmetal skies. Yahrzeit candles nest in pine
trees of Ponary, line the train tracks of Auschwitz, Sobibor,

Bergen-Belsen, Theresienstadt. In his workshop, he
resuscitates peg boxes, fingerboards, weary scrolls. Mother

of pearl inlays are revived for their Stars of David. Each holy
instrument a testimony, their strings learn to quiver again

with vowels that sing from collar bones of legacy for ghosts
of six million mouths that once ached for the ear of God.

Dew Point in Big Sur

At sunrise a condor soars above us,
wind courses past its wingtips, *a dozen
swords swinging through the air*, said
the wildlife photographer—a bird's ancient
job to clean the carcass. Pearly gems
of dew glisten atop my camp tent, another
hymn for fleeting, and the fresh grammar
of deer hoofprints along with low growls
of thunder. Through my ear buds defiance
and sorrow swells from handwritten scores
composed by inmates of Terezin—their
symphonic will to live now breathes into
these moments of dew point, accompanied
by a first quarter moon still lingering.

Immigrant Sisters at the End of the World

Between 1860 and 1939, thousands of poor young women
from Eastern European shtetls were sold into sex slavery
by the Jewish-run Zwi Migdal crime syndicate which controlled
highly profitable brothels in Brazil, Argentina and the U.S.

How to pry open the iris of footnote.
As they stooped around rickety tables
on shtetl dirt floors they imagined an orange
a day and gold capped teeth. So peasant
girls with milky skin and luscious hair
left their hardscrabble homes sleeved
in promise from so many visiting Prince
Charmings in patent-leather shoes,
tailored trousers, and silk handkerchiefs
soaked in rose water to temper poverty's stench.

By ship or train, the new climate of new world
was double-dealing, empty of marriage,
seamstress careers, or taffeta finery. Instead
the air was burdened with fear and sadness,
immigrant streets of trapped women in the many
"convents" of Buenos Aires, Rio de Janeiro, or
New York's Lower East Side. Yoked by greedy
pimps to another kind of assembly line with rape
the often tool of the trade, each Eve did their
bidding, merchandise of the counterfeit kind.

And so the bruised skin of days and nights
began—the who's your daddy in a labyrinth
of rooms with flimsy plywood partitions
in dilapidated clapboard brothels, to feel
the not feeling of lips leeching at their napes,
stale breath of sugarcane alcohol, rough
hands to paw their breasts, pry open
their thighs, the insignificance of release.

These transplanted sisters forced and entered,
counted and discounted, dank scent of lavender
struggling to find its no's.

Forged letters back home to Odessa,
Lodz, Krakow, Kiev. *I'm afraid your daughter
is lost forever. She's a woman who belongs
to everybody now.* Yiddish rhymes from childhood
whispered to soothe their cheap, camisoled sleep.
*I'm a queen who saved her people / She was pretty
and she was smart / If you guessed Queen Esther /
Then you can play the part.* The spit at their heels,
hushed children nudged across cobblestones when
their red lipsticked, heavily rouged, high-heeled clicks
walked by. These colonized flower buds that rotted
in shame and syphilis, beatings and stabbings,
yellow fever, tuberculosis, or desperate swallows
of carbolic acid.

How to heal the script for these women of footnote long gone—
the Bruchas, Rebeccas, Sophias, and Rosas, the Klaras, Olgas,
Lenas and Helenas, the Berthas, Isabels, Rachels, and Fannys.
Today, we perform your *tahara* cleansing your bodies with
cascades of sacred water to comfort and purify you at last.

Soutine Logistics

*The main reason I bought so many of his paintings
was that they were a surprise, if not a shock,
and I wanted to find out how he got that way.*
Albert C. Barnes, art collector,
on painter Chaïm Soutine (1893-1943)

His canvases thaw right before our eyes, ocher into
vermillion, umber into sienna, mixtapes of blood
and guts and flesh. We pay and repay attention
to tumbling mounds of buildings and trees contorted,
landscapes churning with angst. As if Jacob's angel
was pickaxed by impasto. Double outsider, shtetl rayfish
with anguished wings, truth sayer pronouncing
distortion. In portraits, mismatched eyes pause servitude.
In still lifes warrens of Yiddish ulcerate. Plucked goose,
strung pheasants and hares, cows splayed and rendered,
all polestars of slaughter. Near his end, horse and donkey
heads bowed with exhaustion, muffled cries in their
throats. Valorize this reticent Jew, ram tangled in thicket,
life and death shape-shifter schmeared with savior paint.

Love Letter from Ghetto Girl Comedians to 21st Century Offspring

(from Patsy Abbott, Belle Barth, and Pearl Williams)

When a man of 100 can be fertile and a woman of ninety gives birth, Abraham and Sarah let loose laughter into the world. Or so says the Torah. And then it was the 1950s with our dirty records in the basements of parents. We were brazen Jewish jokers working through the stealth of defense while vying for the sacred twinge of chuckling. We knew how to grind and gnaw the bone with freedom to subvert puritanical *goyim*. We were vaudeville's throwbacks—crafting joy in dark places—risqué repertoires with secret codes of Yiddishisms.

We were vulgar and garish, our emblems of honor for any heckler. *Shut your hole, honey. Mine's making money.* You bet we were aging ghetto girls living in margins exotic. We knew how to hold 'em with Borscht Belt rhythms, shaggy dog zany, and salty punchlines that reclaimed our immigrant anxiety and *Oy, vey!* the right to kvetch in sequined gowns and painted eyebrows. To see around the corners of language—there we were victorious, all lusty and fleshy to hurl maniacal schtick in smokey 3am dives or on party LP's under the counter. We were cavernous knishes threatening to swallow up any man with or without foreskin. *What's the definition of coward? It's a man who when he wakes up in his wife's armpit, he's scared to open his eyes.*

So 21st century bitches, we're feeling proud. From inside Mother Matryoshka you strut right out onto the spotlight and swagger up to that mic erect in all its phallic glory. With abrasive winks and spat-out deliveries, your spit-ball jeremiads brim with deft venom. Shebrews front and center flooding packed theaters, streaming your specials, poking at Instagram, podcasts, and TikTok verticals. In pre-gig— your jokes bleed onto cocktail napkins and 7-Eleven receipts. In post-gig—pillowcases full of bees. Hail daughters. We throw packets of super-studded condoms at your feet and cheer your naughty encores.

Somedays Barbie

You favored tender leaves and petals in your summer borsht
and tried to sip strawberry milk through a paper straw
of swirling pink stripes that tickled your perfectly sealed lips.
And sometimes when my index finger and thumb
rubbed into your waist, I dissolved into a field
of stunted wishes. I loved you stupid when you sat
on the wrong side of synagogue taunting all the yarmulke
men and puberty boys who admired you awkward.
And you always forgave me for the dark quiet of your shoe
box bed with thrift-store hankies and cotton ball pillows
because my father wouldn't justify a dream house.
Some days I wanted to break your *shiksa* face open
and bury you out back in the soft earth of my mother's
rock garden where the sun didn't always know
the right amount of warm. Yet there were days
when your story was a song of deep, low sounds
from where you lingered on the far side of mother
star. Under my pillow, o magic sister of fashion prowess,
o forecast whisperer, you made sure I received your dreams
filled with liminal ideas of kiss and matched accessory.
Sometimes we would stretch out on our backs under oaks,
humming to the soft beat of acorns falling near our heads
and the ants dancing between our fingers and we were blissful
as fellow princesses floating down from the clouds. And some
days my brother and I would stuff you into his toy army jeep
and speed you into kitchen walls for the delight of your wig
wardrobes catapulting like drunken bats.

Golda's Having a Dinner Party

They cram through the house gate on Baron Hirsch Street
where in her kitchen, aproned and perspiring, Golda Meir's
at the stove pinching the last powder of paprika into
her pot of chicken soup with kneidlach. *'Welkəm. Erev tov,*
her husky voice flourishes as this band of women from
the dawn take their seats around her green formica table.
No policy initiatives or state secrets tonight, their host
dispatches cheerfully along with spoons and forks for supper,
miniature vases of poppies at each place setting.

The ceiling fan gives Eve a chill so she asks to borrow
one of Golda's shawls as she sits down. *I guess patriarchy
began with me, but I was the "manly" one who took the fruit
of challenge with chin up and eyes clear.* Golda chuckles.
Eve appeals: *Prime Minister, we all know that famous bite
of your coffee blend. Please, a cup with sweet cream
and we can get on to the fulcrum of fear and desire.*

So the rest pull out their chairs and settle in, all figurehead
ancients with faces from algorithms buzzing through minds
of the old masters, as well as Golda's mass media countenance
for a Zionist queen. She places a pot of her brew on the table
along with three bottles of mead. *The old kingdoms linger,*
she declares and the group breaks into snickers and soft
applause. Lot's Wife is in a declarative mood as she lifts
a glass for boasting, *Call me Chloe now. I've claimed
a name and I'm moving forward.*

Between shared triangles of warm pita, Sarah and Hagar
trade melancholy scenes: how hard their sons suckled
their nipples, how the hotbed suite of dogma usurped
their friendship leaving them with calloused feet, how
plotting to kick that hairy father in the nuts could have

been satisfying. From stove to table, table to stove,
Golda's orthopedic shoes and austere bun keep rhythm.
Goldie, we heard you finally declassified your chicken soup
recipe, Rebekah calls out between slurps. *We must have copies*
before we leave. It's delicious and as persuasive as my savory
goat stew delivered with lamb skins of silken hair.
Golda nods for what clandestine persistence can reap.

Slices of honey cake glisten on Desert Rose china
and with shoulders squared, forgiveness is passed
around the table. What androcentric fantasies bared,
entangling Rachel and Leah, Bilhah and Zilpah
(desperate wives, the rapes of enslaved women);
justifying incest for Lot's two daughters (anything
to preserve manhood's lineage); delivering a Jewish
state borne from massive slaughter on a world's stage
(maniacal addiction for power).

Golda's big black American DeSota roars into the driveway
and Deborah bounds into the apartment. *Where's my favorite*
Yiddish socialist? she blurts, clutching a swinging bouquet
of roped salamis. She embraces Golda and they smile into
each other knowing their risky covenants—clash of sabres,
lethal spit of gunfire, two Israeli warriors wedged between
what's at the edge and what's at the center. Moonlight enters
through windows. Deborah takes a seat at the table—all
sisters into the night. Golda and her guests raise their goblets
of bright wine—for dust and divinity, for the difference
between prayer and bold gumption, for time to leap out of
toughened skins that have been gilded for the sake of others.

Reviving Leo

Leo Frank, a Jewish-American pencil factory superintendent,
was convicted in 1913 of the murder of a 13-year-old employee,
Mary Phagan, in Atlanta, Georgia. His trial, conviction, appeals
and lynching by an anti-semitic mob attracted national attention.

[ ]
Could we rewind,
as pencils do what
pencils do best,
and erase smudges
of remarkable circumstance?

Could we rewind,
as pencils do what
pencils do best,
to sketch a Hamsa hand
that resketches itself?

[ ]
Difficult mercy.
Hazard that won't be muzzled.

[ ]
1913. Dixie wanted it all back
and more. Agrarian paradise.
Christian white of it. Mob law.

[ ]
From a Georgian fiddler's anthem:
> *Have a notion in my head,*
> *When Frank he comes to die,*
> *Stand examination*
> *In a court-house in the sky.*

[ ]
How lavender Mary's dress,
how sweet the parasol,
tender the straw hat.
Starlings stirred a centrifuge
into the tangled skies
of Confederate parade.

[ ]
Lungs of abomination,
old language from dark throats.
The manifold profusion
of hot-blood atonement.

[ ]
From Thoreau, your fellow pencil maker:
Rather than love, than money, than fame,
give me truth. Affidavits were warped
with the Jewish Question, the Longest Hatred.
Belief, an enemy of fact.

[ ]
Yahrzeit candles shiver
with shadows of ghost limbs.
It happened before it happened.

[ ]
Opera cinched by the ferrules
of new industry and its sweatshops.
This daughter of poverty with her
hair ribbons and tiny fingers
at the longitude and latitude of metal room,
her work station, erasers into brass bands,
last stage in the process.

[ ]
Sunday morning and a tiny wishbone in her purse.
       Near the basement's coal bin
                 her failed body cindered and grimed.
           Headlines bleed, EXTRA'S leech,
                    inimical power of careless information
       and the din that spectators desire,
                      the credence gained from
mouth to mouth.
Justice abscessed, rule of perjury
          and forensics in erectile dysfunction.
                  Sharksucker prosecutor curating
                      tissues of lies and innuen-
do,
       linguistic fingerprints misleading
                   in the did or done of it,
          the sweeper's tale scrubbed and tailored.
Incompetence a curse
         for this Yankee Jew
             worthy to pay for the crime.
[ ]
Prosecution's courtroom diagram:
       Machine room where murder was committed.
       Course by stairs taken to elevator.
       The elevator shaft.
       Route taken with body to elevator.
       Pencil shavings dump where body was found,
       where lock and staple were pulled from rear door.
       Location of office.
Defense's courtroom diagram:
       Entrance to factory.
       Frank's office. Second floor. Stairway.
       Ground floor chute.
       Elevator shaft.

Basement.
  X where body was found.
Logos fastened with safety pins.

[ ]
Leo, your appeals wandered through the seasons,
each time losing their aim.
Commutation and a governor's burning effigy.
7 and 1/2 inches a butcher knife takes
from your jailed neck. Near miss.

[ ]
Hot August afternoon.
Caravan of tires bump
over 100 miles
of Georgia's red clay.
People have the right
to carry out a verdict.
How to transliterate a world—
snippets of rope and shreds
from your night shirt,
postcard photographs
marketed wide.
Under an oak tree,
the blindfolded eyes
of necessary angels.

Sh'ma, a frilled wound of prayer
to loosen the hangman's coil.
Gazelle, your alter ego
as you shrink your heart,
release bound tendons.
Veins slip through marble walls
of courtrooms, synagogues.
Cloud of your body.
Last breath rises
in quiet rage and rapture.

[ ]
Inside a Brooklyn kitchen,
a mother's hands tremble
as she braids Sabbath bread,
the language of relentless ache.

In Atlanta, light through a widow's
lace curtains speckles the floor.
Widow opens her window,
leans over the ledge.
Wind chimes call you back.
The anima of resurrection
wrapped in elegy, salted
stones on your gravestone,
semper idem.

[ ]
Time says yes,
the day looks right.
You in your perfect suit
and exquisite penmanship
ferried by a dreamlike boat.
Your face pressed into mist,
your sugar skull sparkling,
the moon coming to rest.

Dispatches

after photographs by Frédéric Brenner
from *Diaspora: Homelands in Exile*

In the belly of a Roman amphitheater
nine beardless young Jews in striking
manliness, biker helmets under
their muscular arms,
stand bold with legs apart,
arranged like shiny hubris
of never-scuffed bowling pins,
readied for the gladiators
of an ancient Empire to take
their best shot. Jews old
as the world.

At the end of an alley,
it's Purim in Jerusalem,
shadows calculate
a black hat
in determined stride
through a proscenium.
In foreground, a child
with angel wings
skips atop cankers of stones
and impossible snow.
Esther's folktale delivers
to alley saints what's
tied up with a thorny bow—
annihilation can be averted
if one is pretty enough
and savvy enough to coerce
a ruler's scepter tip
for bending hope and history
towards justice.

▶

The male corpus
of three outstretched arms
parallel, flexed, and extended from
right to left like a Hebrew equal sign
demanding *Look.*
This convoy of three defiant faces
with bushy brows and three clenched
fists, like prayer beads circling
the tattooed horror of *Never Forget.*
And at the far left a fourth man
wearing the dignity of infinite
sorrow, his tired eyes, his left hand
shielding his wrinkled, other cheek.

▶

At the weary study house,
among an excess of huddled men
in Russian fur hats and prayer caps,
a boy calls you with his eyes
from a bench of slumped brethren
nodding off. Around him so many
gestures in Torah or newspaper debate
at candlelit tables beneath curtains
sagging and torn. And this boy—
stranded in the scrim of tradition,
his restless head tilted ever so
slightly, his palms sturdy on his knees,
as if to say *this stale air won't keep
me long in mind or matter.*

▶

Seven Russian barbers waist-deep
in the Dead Sea, claiming
and claimed by the rhyming
of razors. Heads of sheeted
clients float above their laps.
The tatting of salt on their fingers,
stones in their pockets, this postcard
by proxy for the grooming
of promise that milk and honey
will seep into shaving mugs
of resettlement.

We recognize her compiled self
in the smooth, stone lap
of a Yemeni alcove,
this robed woman,
intimate text in diagonal.
Perfect folds of her robe
beguile, the suppose
of her naked toe pointing,
the wealth of predicates
in her turbaned gaze
only for us. This place
she has taken at the climax
of your thread that glitters
with invisible jewels.

What they are and what
they are not. Tight across
the frame, a minyan of rabbinical
women lined up with each other,
all wrapped in *tallis* and binding

prayer gear. They seem resolved
in elliptical splendor—tall, short,
back-turned or shoulder leaning,
heads bold with hairstyles, each
a proud note on this musical
scale of defiance.

How many Grouchos
does it take to fill
the nooks and crannies
of a Marxist funhouse?
4 to a row and 4 squared.
Enough caterpillar eyebrows
to circle the moral freight
of Kafkaesque absurdities.
A suite of mustaches, each
a runway for immigrant angst,
and an army of cigars wagging
from too much big city ghetto,
slim odds for a sitcom today.

To certify the flesh
of what had been,
bare chests of cycloped
mastectomies seated
at a long table, coiffed
Americans with tender
hands entwined, their eyes
locked on us to pronounce
womanhood still, Ashkenazi
triumph, *Kinehora*.

Two pyramids debate
on a Las Vegas strip:
Pristine lines of history's cruel
architecture, exploited glory
in deep shadow of a luxury hotel
versus a human triangle
of 120 young Jews stacked
in academy uniforms and sunshine,
their soulful pyramid grinning.
What to make of staging?
What to make of servitude
to the lords of mise-en-scène
and this kingdom of light?

Shepherd's Cento

She's a clairvoyant of human vapor,
the grey spine of a pencilled world.

She straightened up slowly, plaited her hair
and wound it tight around her head.
"Do you know where you are?" she asks.

Clouds break and gather
like the joining hands of prayer.
What the gleaners leave in the corners
shrouded in the winds' shawl.

The prophet works hard at dreaming
on a pillow of moonlight.
Let's make up stories out of stars
or perhaps just a match
set to a wick of pure olive oil.

Words can split the sea
the word and the non-word
manifesto stitching the air.

In the flimsy house of logic
a magician finds quarters
behind our ears
like small spectral windows
in a golden tower.

And perhaps the kabbalah was right:
it's all a tending.
Like some green or mauve
swath laid down on canvas.

The minor key. The tragic violin
and exuberant clarinet,
pasture sheep and
their singing wool
the ribbed leaf a spot of scarlet floats
on the shivering creek,
poems direct as what the birds said.

50

Isolated thinkers at pasture
grazing the rich meadows,
unspoken questions, how they echo,
a voice that looks for its throat.

A lifetime pushing a tiny grain,
the blue path never curves—
opened for a few fluorescent minutes,
born into the tribe of time,
will vanish into its blurring distance
like a dress you wear only once,
by the sea, guided guided away,
guided and guided away.

With gratitude to Sean Singer, Eleanor Wilner, Patricia Averbach,
Charles Reznikoff, Nelly Carol V. Davis, Nelly Sachs, Rose Drachler,
Philip Levine, Joy Ladin, Rachel Neve-Midbar, Maya Bernstein, Michael
Heller, Emily Light, Henry Shukman, Ilya Kaminsky, Celia Dropkin,
Philip Terman, Sam Taylor, Hannah Stephenson, Charlene Fix, Alicia
Suskin Ostriker, Denise Levertov, Gerald Stern, Louise Glück, Marcia
Falk, Yerra Sugarman, Alan Shapiro, Ben Lerner, Maya Pindyck, Jane
Hirshfield, Matthew Zapruder, Gertrude Stein.

Waffle House

Before the thing of cell phones
                              & after a stuffed toilet left
          to late-night running, we were witnesses
                              for *in medias res* as it careened
from a cackling pack of Boilermakers hurling Jew slurs.   White-
haired Cook
              launches a spatula in oiled motion of call & response
                        then shower of spit, flung salt & pepper shakers
                    smeared platters of happy logos Frisbeed across the
counter
                              stink bugs like raisins on steamed
windows
                    moths outside twirling under yellow,
                                        red flashing in
parking lot,
tableau of our thinking too-late-for-escape.
          Boilermakers seething in paddy wagon,
                              ducktails streaked with oleo.
              Handcuffed Cook, weary lion in jaundiced light,
                                        aching to erase the
world
                                                  and pop
god
                                                            in
jail

instead

Stand-Up Ghazal

It's wandered through the ages, that tell-tale levity of punchline.
Agent against darkness, every cave fire's flickering punchline.

Two shlemiels walk into a bar up to their eyeballs with angst &
kvetching, then flip-side pivot forgives with luminous punchline.

Kick Me signs slapped onto their backs, a millennia of persecution,
irritations that rankle and arrest, all holy grail of punchline.

Pacing & fisted mic as confessional, another formula for funny.
Self-deprecation cuts both ways, pithy punching bag of punchline.

Rabbi, priest, & imam slouch together on a rickety park bench,
Is jokester really joking? The slippery subtext of punchline.

Dr. Freud, you've splayed me onto your threadbare couch to lay
bare my cracks in my cracking up from hurled & ruthless punchlines.

Monet and Manet + Liebermann + Hitler

A painter paints a painter.

Another painter purchases the painting.

A failed painter mounts a genocide of biblical proportion.

A failed painter paints atrocity into acts of brutal thievery.

A postscript paints the further story:

> Monet's *Manet painting in Monet's Garden* (1874) was confiscated
> by the Nazis from a Berlin apartment in March 1943 along with other
> belongings of Martha Liebermann (widow of painter/collector Max)
> following her suicide to avoid deportation to a concentration camp.
> After it was seized and inventoried on behalf of the Gestapo, it has not
> been seen since.

A painting retreats to the secret garden of imagination

                                   where it began.

Religion

The Dude was here
The Dude's a saint
Saints pick their teeth
Saints spread like wildfire
Wildfire eats oxygen
Wildfire purifies
Purify your thoughts
Purify your chant
Chant for Godtopia
Chant for redemption
Redemption for massacre
Redemption for torture
Torture to convert
Torture to believe
Believe in deep alchemy
Believe that heretics will confess
Confess your Inquisition
Confess Blood Libels
Libel the doubter of blood into wine
Libel discounter of walks on water
Water down kosher
Water limp family trees
Tree farms for Christmas
Tree bountiful for original sin
Sin for whence thou comest
Sin for uttering Allah or *Oy Vey*
Oy vey to suicide bombers
Oy vey to Middle East carnage
Carnage for those to keep Sabbath
Carnage for those to be pretty and Gay
Gay for will against will
Gay for propaganda tweets
Tweet for apocalypse
Tweet for immigrant *schnorrers*

Schnorrers in ethnic food trucks
Schnorrers who want piece of the pie
Pie-in-the-face comedians jabbing
Pie in the heavenly sky
Sky with old bearded man
Sky crowded with prayers
Prayers to combat nothingness
Prayers for desperate mercy
Mercy can heal
Mercy in golden rule
Rule equals upper hand
Rule the State with religion
Religion that takes
Religion that gives
Gives
Takes

Judeophobia*

*Dr. Leon Pinsker, who coined the word in 1882 in his argument for a Zionist state, explained the term this way: *As a psychic aberration, it is hereditary, and as disease transmitted for two thousand years, it is incurable.*

squall of thorns \ flood of rotting teeth \ cabinet of lost lungs \ shuttle-cock bloodied \ womb imploded \ serpents in the waters \ tattoo drenched with saliva \ bird wing wrenched from its socket \ salt-caked flesh \ ulcer in fault line \ punchline trapdoors \ assembly line for iron muzzles \ wishbone jagged \ glass splinters in the stew \ headlines impotent \ footnotes spider-webbed with sorrow \ lemon-sick scent of bleach \ hard mathematics \ terrorist snake burrows \ dance party death trap \ gleeful snuff footage \ fossilized cures lodged in riverbeds \ exile exiled \ two-headed, victim|persecutor \ petition petition the ghosts

My Father's Trees

after Hamas, after Gaza

In Israel a ring of trees
encircle his legacy, memorial
from his bowling buddies
almost four decades ago.
The certificate declared from
Leviticus: *When you come
to the land, you shall plant trees.*
My father never visited that land,
and neither have I, but I trust
his trees are there still
in the Negev Desert, perhaps
a family arborctum of carob,
pear, redbud, almond,
cypress, olive, oak.

Bologna sauce is what my father
cooed that he'd squeeze out of me
when his hugs were hymns
in gratitude for finally finding
the good life with wife, daughter, son.
His ideas of assimilated Jewish
migrated to my secular shaping.
Synagogue only on high holidays,
Sabbath just another Friday night
for cheeseburgers and *Hogan's Heroes.*
And Zionist? He was more B'nai Brith
bowling league and temple dues.

Now I imagine his Israeli trees
forsaken by milk and honey. Their roots
sponging up bloodshed. Their skins
trembling with gunfire and bomb blast.

Their bent architecture davening
a shameful Kaddish with barren,
fractal branches reaching
reaching for nothing but air.

Custody

I'm trying to swallow light
sort major from minor
invite people over for supper
pause to relish vibration
Persian kneading my chest
jouissance dripping into
my thirsty cup
hoofbeats in my ear

Moonlight on a cheek
never precise enough
even when my Fiat rumbles
through the rainbow
that bends down
to a wet road
tenderness thrills
alertness unfastens
what tunnels under rocks
yet feeble deceit in summary

Who had first thought
first nod
first murmur
sometimes we are simpering wounds
sometimes prayer
the sugar and salt of memory
our remainder goods

Chiffon logic
dresses the question
gestures in the right direction
nights of the planets
seasons fusing
into one another
good luck amulets declaring
skin's thin veil

to balance on the ledge
where quicksilver parts yearn
to corkscrew towards whole

Dreams free me of time
winds anchor me
to moment
the in & out of
persistent chatter
secret winks
what to read
in the waiting room
how much can
an answering machine
really answer
stains
that forever stain
no days back

Ancient mercies linger
timeworn libraries
of martyrs
tardy redeemers
words cling to doorposts
that give up nothing
but dust
restless whorls of breath
from believers
stories within
stories
no way
to know
denouement
one minute breeds
another.

A Ubiquity of Blue

Lapis lazuli on my tongue
        prayer
for bright, clear skies
           however blue a blue may be—
              David's blue star
                  billowing.

From deep recesses
        opalescent blue hands
bejeweled with purity
        to repel the servitude
           of evil eyes.

Kitchen window
        cerulean with moonbeams
Yahrzeit candle
        flickering all night
           whispering
              your name.

Think blue—a value
        of darkness or
under your feet
        a reverie
of brickwork
        sapphire sacred.

Weary of an ancient world
        frayed blue threads
of Papa's prayer shawl
        tucked inside
           memory's drawer.

Rods and cones dazzled—
        breezy fields

of spring bluebells
      turquoise stomps
of blue-footed boobies
      my husband's gaze
a wordless trust
        that renders
          sky and sea.

Rock and Redeemer

In the shepherd's dream of the world, a pasture
of blushing sand that froths in ebb and flow.
Suspended megaliths like sentinels
ship their shadows across landscape in majesty
of infinite progression.   Praise sky
that holds clouds like soft flour.   Praise melody
of silence and sunlight.   Praise faith
that defies gravity, our most ancient language.

IN GRATITUDE

Thank you to all the generous editors of journals who believed in these poems and delivered them into the world. My deep gratitude to the following writers who gift me with friendship and feedback, always knowing just when to push and just when to pull: Sayuri Ayers, Sandy Berman, Kathleen Burgess, Sandra Feen, Charlene Fix, Rebe Huntman, Louise Robertson, Mikelle Hickman-Romine, Chuck Salmons and all the good folks from the Salon and Bistro writing groups. I am indebted to Carol V. Davis, Charlene Fix, Bonnie Proudfoot, Hannah Stephenson, and Phil Terman for the grace of their time and attention and for the artistry of their words to frame the energy of this collection. Much gratitude to sweet friend and artist Hani Hara who so willingly agreed to lend his painting for the book's cover. And of course, thank you Eileen Clearly and the entire Lily Poetry Review Press team for rendering this collection with such artfulnesss and integrity, and for the life and work of poet Paul Erwin Nemser in whose memory my collection humbly carries on his legacy through his book award.

ACKNOWLEDGMENTS

"A Ubiquity of Blue" (**The Deronda Review**)

"Bagel Lady in Night" (**Last Stanza**)

"Collector" (**The Inflectionist Review**)

"Cradling Time" (**Penumbra**)

"Crosshatching" (**Gasconade Review**)

"Custody" (**Cold Signal**)

"Dear Chiva and Rikel" (**Bicoastal Review**)

"Dear Isaac and Joseph" (**Lily Poetry Review**)

"Dew Point in Big Sur" (**Bicoastal Review**)

"Dispatches" (**The Klecksograph**)

"From Sister Namesake" (**Gordon Square Review**)

"Golda's Having a Dinner Party" (**Kairos Literary Magazine**)

"Hide & Seek" (**Gyroscope Review**)

"How to Make A Picture Book For The Soul That You Miscarried" (**Penumbra**)

"Immigrant Sisters at the End of the World' (**Burningword Literary Journal**)

"The Interfacings of Henry Miller and My Uncle Saul" (**Broad Street**)

"Jewcat" (**The Paradox Magazine**)

"Judeophobia" (**The Deronda Review**)

"Kosher" (**Black Horse Review**)

"Leavings" (**Stone Poetry Journal**)

"Love Letter from Ghetto Girl Comedians to 21st Century Offspring" (**The Los Angeles Press**)

"Luthier" (**One Art**)

"Monet and Manet + Liebermann + Hitler" (**Poetica Review**)

"My Father's Trees" (**New Verse News**)

"My Friend's Chagalls" (**Ekphrasis Magazine**)

"Of Steamship Steerage" (**Gordon Square Review**)

"Packing With Lilith" (**Muleskinner Journal**)

"Religion" (**2023 New Generation Beats Anthology from National Beat Poetry Foundation**)

"Reviving Leo" (**The Seraphic Review**)

"Rock and Redeemer" (**Cold Signal**)

"Shepherd's Cento" **(The Klecksograph)**

"Shepherd's Hour" **(Amethyst Review)**

"Shofar" **(Rappahannock Review)**

"Somedays Barbie" **(Bryant Literary Review)**

"Soutine Logistics" **(Cold Signal)**

"Stand Up Ghazal" **(The Paradox Magazine)**

"Suburban Trajectory" **(Rough Cut Press)**

"Sway of Perennial" **(Ballast Journal)**

"Uncle Max's Deli" **(U.S.1 Worksheets)**

"Vegan Dreams of Meat" **(Ship of Fools)**

"Waffle House" **(Triggerfish Critical Review)**

"What We Carry" **(Creation Magazine)**

"When Auntie Kissed a Beat" **(Slipstream)**

"You Were Here" **(Gasconade Review)**

"Zemirot" **(The Nashville Review)**

GLOSSARY

Ashkenazi—a Jewish person of Central or Eastern European descent

bimah—raised platform in a synagogue from which services are led and the Torah is read

chasid—member of a strictly orthodox Jewish sect

dreidel—four-sided spinning top for Chanukah celebrations

gimel—letter that stands for take all in the dreidel game

golem—from Jewish folklore, a giant clay figure brought to life by magic to protect the Jewish people

goyim— non-Jewish people

High Holidays—Jewish holy days of Yom Kippur and Rosh Hashanah

kabbalah—an esoteric method, discipline and school of thought in Jewish mysticism

kinehora—an expression said to ward off the evil eye or bad luck in general; it is a contraction of three Yiddish words: kayn ayin hara, literally "not (kayn) the evil (hara) eye (ayin)"

klezmer—traditional Eastern European Jewish music

kneidlach—Yiddish term for matzo balls

knishes—dumpling of dough with a filling

kosher—the preparation of food according to the requirements of Jewish law

Kol Nidre—prayer sung on Yom Kippur, Day of Atonement

midrash—a Jewish mode of interpretation that not only engages the words of the text, but also behind the text, and beyond the text.

minyan—a quorum of ten men over the age of 13 required for traditional Jewish public worship

pogrom—organized massacres of the Jews in Russian and Eastern Europe during late 19th and early 20th century

Purim—Jewish holiday commemorating the saving of the Jews from massacre recounted in the Book of Esther

putz—silly fool

rebbe—rabbi, religious leader

shiksa—gentile girl or woman

shtetl—small Jewish village in Eastern Europe

shul—synagogue

siddur—Jewish prayer book

tallis/tallit—a fringed garment worn as a prayer shawl by religious Jews

tahara—a Jewish ritual cleansing of the deceased

tref—ritually unclean or unfit according to Jewish law. opposed to kosher

Welkəm. Erev tov—"Welcome, Good Evening" in Hebrew

yenta—gossip or busybody

zemirot—a Jewish hymn

About the author

Rikki Santer's poetry has been published widely and has received many honors including Pushcart and Ohioana book award nominations, a fellowship from the National Endowment for the Humanities, and in 2023 she was named Ohio Poet of the Year. She is a member of the teaching artist roster of the Ohio Arts Council and a past vice-president of the Ohio Poetry Association. She has had published seven full-length poetry collections and seven chapbook sequences exploring such topics as the Hopewell earthworks of Newark, Ohio; the late Kahiki Supper Club of Columbus, Ohio; the art of ventriloquism, the complex world of fashion, and the TV series Twilight Zone. Her collection, *Resurrection Letter,* dedicated to surrealist artist Leonora Carrington, was grand prize short-listed for the Eric Hoffer Book Award, and *Shepherd's Hour* won the Paul Nemser Book Prize from Lily Poetry Review Books. Please contact her through her website https://rikkisanter.com